Discover Helicopters

by Calee M. Lee

© 2012 by Calee M. Lee
Hardcover ISBN: 978-1-5324-3724-3
Paperback ISBN: 9781623950392
eISBN: 9781623953140
Images licensed from Fotolia.com
All rights reserved.
No portion of this book may be reproduced without express permission of the publisher.
First Edition
Published in the United States by Xist Publishing
www.xistpublishing.com

2

Helicopters are different from other types of aircraft.

They can take off and land vertically, hover for extended periods of time and move at low airspeeds.

This makes them ideally suited for a wide range of tasks that cannot be performed by other types of aircraft.

Helicopters can be used for transportation, construction, fire fighting, search and rescue and tourism.

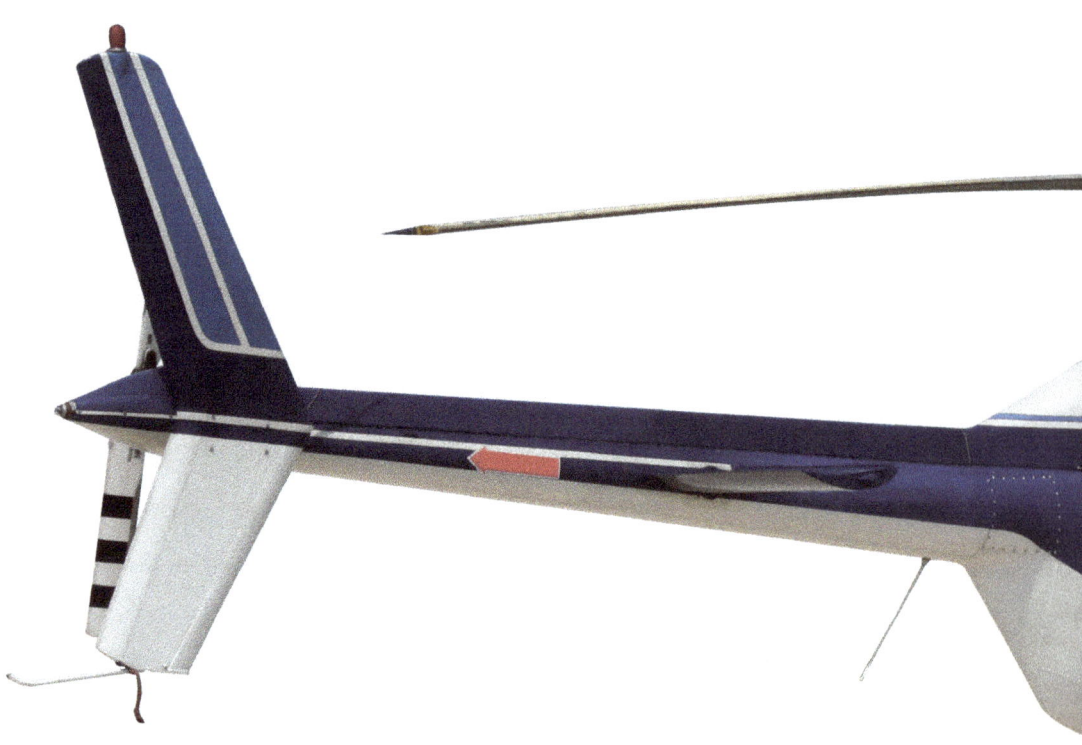

Helicopters are very useful but they are one of the most difficult types of aircraft to fly.

Helicopters are used by the military. This army helicopter has guns for going into enemy territory.

Police departments and other law enforcement agencies use helicopters to pursue suspects.

They often coordinate with officers on the ground to report suspects' locations and movements.

Rescue helicopters are used to save people in remote locations. They also transport people to hospitals.

Helicopters come in a wide range of colors. Bright colors, like red, make is easy to spot a helicopter in the sky.

This attack helicopter is painted black so it can fly missions at night and not be seen.

Military helicopters can be painted with camouflage to help make them more difficult to detect.

The camouflage is different depending on the area where the helicopter will be flying.

13

There are many different controls used to fly a helicopter.

A pilot must be able to do different things with his or her right and left hands and both feet at the same time.

Helicopters do not fly as fast or as high as fixed-wing planes. They are best for navigating tight spaces or going short distances at low altitude.

Some helicopters are very small and are designed to hold only a pilot and one passenger.

These helicopters are often used to train pilots.

Very large helicopters need two sets of rotors. This Boeing CH-47 Chinook is the most common type of dual-rotor helicopter.

Larger helicopters are designed to transport many passengers. Can you guess how many rows of passengers will fit in this helicopter?

Here's a hint: count the windows and double your answer.

20

This is the rotor system for a helicopter. The rotor is made up of a mast, hub and rotor blades.

The mast is the metal pole that connects to the helicopter body.

The hub is where the rotor blades connect to the mast.

The rotor blades spin very quickly to make the helicopter move.

This is the tail rotor of a helicopter.

It counteracts the main rotor on top of the helicopter to help provide lift and thrust. Thrust is the force that makes the helicopter move forward through the air.

Even if the engine stops, the helicopter's rotor will continue to spin so the helicopter can glide safely to the ground.

This is another kind of tail rotor. It is called a fantail and is quieter and safer than a conventional tail rotor.

On the back of this helicopter, there is a steel guard to protect the tail rotor from ground strikes. People must be very careful when walking near helicopters.

Helicopters are often used to travel to places where there is nowhere to land a plane.

Because they do not require a runway and can land and take off from very small spaces, helicopters make it possible for people to quickly travel to remote destinations.

Helicopters can have different types of landing gear. This helicopter has skids, which look a bit like skis for landing on flat places.

This helicopter has wheels for landing. It allows the helicopter to takeoff much like an airplane. It also makes for a much softer landing.

This military transport helicopter has retractable wheels. When it lands, it can taxi into a hanger and unload its gear.

Helicopters can hover in the air to stay in one place for an extended period of time. To do this, the pilot must constantly adjust the controls to keep the helicopter aloft and hovering.

www.ingramcontent.com/pod-product-compliance
Lightning Source LLC
Chambersburg PA
CBHW052129150426
42813CB00077B/2672